# Prop Rockery

AKRON SERIES IN POETRY

Titles published since 2003.
For a complete listing of titles published in the
series, go to www.uakron.edu / uapress / poetry

# Prop Rockery

Emily Rosko

The University of Akron Press
Akron, Ohio

Copyright © 2012 by Emily Rosko

All rights reserved • First Edition 2012 • Manufactured in the United States of America. All inquiries and permission requests should be addressed to the Publisher, the University of Akron Press, Akron, Ohio 44325–1703.

16   15   14   13   12             5   4   3   2   1

LIBRARY OF CONGRESS CATALOGING-IN-PUBLICATION DATA
Rosko, Emily, 1979–
Prop rockery / Emily Rosko. — 1st ed.
p. cm. — (Akron series in poetry)
Includes bibliographical references.
ISBN 978-1-937378-15-8 (hardcover : alk. paper) — ISBN 978-1-937378-16-5 (pbk. : alk. paper)
I. Title.
PS3618.O84425P76 2012
811′.6—dc23

2011050857

The paper used in this publication meets the minimum requirements of ANSI / NISO Z39.48–1992 (Permanence of Paper). ∞

Cover: *C'mere Little*, by Aggie Zed, pastels & ink, copyright © 2011. Used with permission. Cover design: Amy Freels

*Prop Rockery* was designed and typeset in Dante and printed on sixty-pound natural and bound by BookMasters of Ashland, Ohio.

# Contents

# Acknowledgments

Sincere thanks to the editors of the literary journals where many of these poems first appeared: *Agni, Barn Owl Review, The Beloit Poetry Journal, The Cincinnati Review, Crazyhorse, Cutbank, The Denver Quarterly, Diode, Front Porch, Hubbub, The Laurel Review, Pank Magazine, Pleiades, Redivider, The Rumpus, Shenandoah*, and *Verse Daily*.

This book was shaped and informed by many, and I would like to thank my colleagues at Cornell University and the College of Charleston and my advisors at the University of Missouri: Scott Cairns, William Kerwin, Raymond Marks, David Read, and especially Lynne McMahon and Sherod Santos for their steadfast support. For their continued friendships, old and new, my gratitude goes to Alice Fulton, Phyllis Janowitz, Nina Liu, and Aggie Zed.

Highest thanks to Mary Biddinger, Amy Freels, John Gallaher, and the University of Akron Press. Thank you, Natasha Sajé. Finally, without my family and Anton, I would have no song to sing.

# Prologue

Where does this start?
>    *Earth underground, the root-veined loam.*

What's the scene?
>    *Any square or expanse.*

What do we do?
>    *Conglomerate, calcify, cave in.*

How did it come to this?
>    *The syllables found us rounded.*

What's the petition to say?
>    *We're for more jag. Less court.*

And if there's no answer?
>    *Off to the bigwigs.*

How will the king be known?
>    *By the worms and fleas.*

What's the flip-side of the sun?
>    *A Caesar-crowned ass, the zero, the melt.*

What can be said for us?
>    *We're slow. We're permanent.*

When's the players' cue?
>    *When the goat song kicks in.*

How does the song go?
>    *Better a bucket for the ham,*
>    *a stool for the scrub. . . .*

[ I ]

# Prop Rockery

We were thinking of starting a band,
all lined up like ducks in a shooting gallery.

This one would be gem, that one
metamorphic, the rest pebbles and some

laboratory-grown, semi-precious stones. The trees
were in it for the long-run; they swayed or stood

stoic, sheltered what they could. We made the cast
as an idle grouping: we played the trump, the idiot,

the glue. We backdropped with hearts hardly
beating, our eyes set straight in our heads: the bombed-

out school kids, the oilfields scrubbed in turns. We chewed
the fat amongst ourselves. You said, this place

should be more festive: a lightning bolt, a snail, a fraud. I set
a crumb aside for the local roof rat; you tallied the droppings,

the amputees, the gold. I blew my top when you lost
"Dominion." You said, what can be done? It's gone,

it's gone. Wind started in through the rift-way, buzzed
over our slate-blue bones. All the leaves have aged

with kindness, all our pretend
looped and windowed raggedness went largely

unseen. We were on stage the whole performance, held
our breath for the final moments with cheeks rent

and red. No neck was slit on our backs; no distraught
lover jumped from our cliff's edge. There was a stirring backstage

we could sense it: a temptress, some anger, some
sin. Weeds came thick around us. The act

had been bungled sorely. We withheld our opinions, sat in wait.
We were good for a throwing.

# [In thy dumb action will I be as perfect]

It all became wait. Tolerate the conditions,
the too and the much.
                             It was a drippy mix
of sensations, a blood-for-beans mentality
from the start.
                             We were bustled up
with pomp, the flashing of rhetoric, the proper
rites carried out to a tee.

   I was bottom-feeder, I was bunk.
   I delivered the sure-footed their forecasts,
     doctored to their sure-footed forecasting needs.

A win-win for the disingenuous, a sore
for the mal at ease.
                             What matter that the high
heavens spoke *law*, that reason relied on
the flimsiness of appeal?
                             We applauded it,
glassy-eyed with doting; in turn, we were shaven,
truncated, unadorned.

   I went *bad shot* to *mouth*, elemental as salt.
   I was a long line of
   example, not first to be put-to-show.

Stone-set time of the tilling fields, row
of sharps and picks.
                             The in-sweep,
the overfill. "That which plucks the fowls"
that stirred the dust.
                             Sing, shifty earth,
the dirt reminds me of the evil I am.

# [All with me's meet that I can fashion fit]

Came down unlettered, wasn't a jot
in the books. A collared name—nature's
crown and rot. The sky had a look
of impasse—calcified, great dividing
glass. With you, you're the long equation;
with me, a fitter for the reed. 'Twas a fine
case study for the moralists, all's foppery
of moss and claim. We dressed to code.
As expected, we became statuary for the lawn.
I put on my drawing-room manners, thus
nickeled, thus brandied, preened
and primed. This clownery's unaccustomed.
The stake is in the land. For clarity's sake,
you be the automatic, and I'll be the ram.

# And So It Was Done Riding the Horse Backward

Insults thrown—as a horse the rider. No damage
but to one's own. Licked to the ground. Mud laced
with roots. Shook out misdirection, took a head

to the mare's ass. A clearer view beyond. Wind spurts
and parts. I'm no bigger than a nickel, worthy
of what's coming. Something like a screen

to a filter, a muzzle to a bit. A discarded oilcloth
that retains the sweat-bent face. The ugly
underneath. Oh, taper me for a candle,

fire-spooked, all lit to an end. A basket's worth
of eggs. Coddle me for a ride. The chickadees
are paired and bibbed, and it's known there'll be

a sucker's piece aside me. For all the young
in their beds, for all the unassuming flock in
the nubby field, here's a little song for your pains.

# Troupe Song

*Beggars, actors, buffoons, and all that tribe.*
—Horace

Our ride took the shape of an old whinny,
all temper and steeled, stayed
but for the kick and the hay. Not

to be hitched. It was a maddening
method, an exercise for the muscle,
a wayfarer's way for us three. We walked

the long haul. Him as the makeshift, me
as the sap, you as the heroine properly voiced
with accord. Falsity's icon: rein

and shoe. All for play and no
transport, though we jigged our own
terrible message—plague and drought

to your crown and thorn. Golden trifle
over-handled. Oh, you're good
for something I hope! A bitchery

of bags to travel with! All the wisdom
says the strong head only flattens
the pillow, but they'll go ga-ga

over the sepia dye tones of your hair,
your canary feebleness—a little tap and tune
adjusted for the count. One, two, three....

The dancer's toes remain the ugliest instrument.

# [Like boys unto a muss kings would start forth]

The pieces as scattered sent the scavengers
to their knees. Fists aflight with each inch
reached for. And what for? A small reward

in rewording. The up-starts and flabby-
jacks scoured the place clean. Grab-bag
of circumstances, a happy misquote, roll

call of life's notarized deeds. I'm sick
to my heels. I'm a sorry doggy-dog day.
They handed out to their liking—

scraps and post-invitations. And I'm
gate-lorn, game for a score. Brushed
up on my curtsey, no less a book

to be recited with my *après vous*, thank
you kindly, most honored, dear,
dear sir. You'll be shin-sore, quite

a target for wits and epigrams. Classy
graffiti, jokes, and riddle-dee-dee.
That's a move. If that's the piece

to pawn for a distempered queen,
then the short game would dub none
king. Hands and blades, flowers

and powers. Should we settle?
Should we mold in the stale
hours of whip, of scratch, of

hound-horn, rabbit, and jack?
I'm not up for study. I'm no case
to be won. You dig holes

in your own ground. Sunk low.
Here we are: tumped over by
humbuggery. Caught neck-and-neck

in a drop-dead race to catch a third.

# [Time and the hour runs through the roughest day]

It's a fishery of looks that swallows us,
squared away in our fenced-off station.
Cypress as sentry, an entanglement straight
to the gully: sharp-toothed wild vine and

bindweed. To the lifeline, a knife:
a clearing away of excess, the short
stick, the hogwash, the tit for tat. You,
with your insider's word; I, with a stumbler's

gaited mouth. Fireside, shadows turn clocks
around your face. We're two
for the time. You're a window; I'm a floor,
dense as a diamond-within-coal, clotted

as new-spun felt. The muddy plains of the heart.
The acres we've crossed, the acres we have not.

# [So that they seeme, and covet not to be]

Nature was written all over it.
An image held. Lead-lined

back to the greenish forest
glass, an estranged view.

The world was swelling.
It was as though the sun

had lent a soiled shadow
brush to each ending.

The drawn so shaped
as fruit, silver-cast

and smoke. We were no
longer alone. Above, birds

to say to us how small
the eye an instrument,

how substantial the
cruelty we deliver each

day. You yourself the one
etched back in crystal.

Reflection without
effort, no longer a clouded

aspect to be worked through.
Time was harder than the rocks.

I could not live without you
to show me my disgrace.

[ II ]

# [Accoutred as I was I plungèd in]

Slippery slope of affects. I wetted
the words, armed to the teeth.
I bled first from the eye, then from

my small heart down. There was a crowd
tapped to nerve, the air fevered, the fitful
clouds turned and turned. A particular

front, a gold-hoard, a going-at-it
with the right dagger. So move to please,
butter their ears, take feeling to fight.

That Art flocked.
That multitude was plucked.
The occasion showcased the swank,

put to a palm-greasing, made it tongue to
tongue to tongue among the rats. A toast
to masstige for all. I broke hand

to foot, I measured amiss. No place
for song or anything noteworthy.
Thus, the action stymied the form:

the swoop and curve, the cross
and diagonal. Disarmed by all points.
The cause was the blame.

I ran myself through.

# Jib Riddle

When reputation becomes the glass
through which others view, there
a blushed face with eyes askew:

the self a thing less one part
we knew. As when a coin
replaces the tongue (false toll

for safe passage), it makes
no impression. So we borrow
ourselves some plumes. Donned,

there might be answers, the silt
stirred up, the waters' muddied
run. Trust's an anchor

but a faulty one. Any upset will
do. It could be glass pressed
with lip-prints, a tip

or a stumble. Curtain for wits
or a shot for the cheaper. We've
swallowed the rougher: gallon

to whale. The rigging's the steady,
some garb we're well-geared
for—as any ladder a rank, as any

height a shallow. The hook
to the punch, the brow furled
in delicate matters. The situation

is seasonal: the willow a full-
blown liar, banked along
the shore, showing slips

of yellow. A turn is a cue, a quiet
full of drown. Work we've cut:
a nose for a face, a price for a loss.

The bone, knot, cloth. Some fat
hog to be bled. Figured. A whole
volume never by chance to be said.

# Tract Song

*What is truth? said jesting Pilate;*
*and would not stay for an answer.*
—Francis Bacon

A bit for a horse, a shoe for a clod
that waits on the muddied road that takes
its time to wind to the town. Carries itself
full of itself. Alongside, the swamp,
murky secret pressed down: sedimental
remains. The stuff of the earth runs
in the brain. It's a feat
disguised as a wind-washed stone;
it's a form to overmaster. No error
in the cattail's fruit, the leaves
that make a seat to suit. A small
shred—no, a large fill beyond
comparison. In the center, in
the outside. I'm forgone. I'm for sale.

# Mare's Nest

*The closer the look one takes at a word, the greater
the distance from which it looks back.*
        —Karl Kraus

Short supply. The machinery's in
rust and web. Any old stamp for pounding

bone to meal. Dried-out trees rubbed to
scrub by the hinds of a horse (a horse

can destroy a field). Tango at the watering
hole, land-rights, a squat,

a cock, a skip-to-my-Lou. NO TRESPASSING,
not one square inch to graze.


                                *Hark, hark, the dogs bark.*
                                *The beggars are coming to town.*


        I was shaken as salt. I was
        as industrial as a drill. Oh pity-poor

        fractured me, brain-way-sided, boring
        through and through, full of ballas and glue.


        ("Jesus, what a bitchy little spinster," so said D. of E.)


                                *Some in rags and some in tags*
                                *and some in silken gowns.*

Overall, the gang was juiced, their sights on
the mustang herd. Honesty's a brute;

the steed's side says M E AT . Razor-wire
rigged across the range, set for trip.


     I got to play scout, the ding-dong
     bell-ringer. I took the binocs, the hook,

     a lucky shoe. Had my watch in the radio
     steel tower; got owl-crossed, got assed

     fast, pulled a switcheroo. The whole charade's
     been arranged as presented: the cow

     pies, the triad, the blank afternoon.


                        *Some gave them white bread,*
                        *and some gave them brown.*


They had helicopters and GPS, all that
cowboy whoopi ti yi yo. The pretty

horses go round (thumpety-thump).
Mowed them

down with tranquilizers (thump), legs
wrapped and bound.


     I duke me up, I talk West. Lost
     my partner, what'll I do?

*And some gave them a good horsewhip*
*and sent them out of the town.*

So then the lines went crack.
"Not to commend, but to set it."

So then went the cleaving, the horses
in a stall for study. I looked at and at.

If left to roam, if overblown,
a horse can destroy a field....

# [The world is deceived with ornament]

All for a table to set the chair,
all for the window to survey
the scene. All for the pen from feather
from flight's air. All for the grass, all

for the moon—a face not named,
its too-rough edges hewn. The trade
of looks, one coin to one's coin grew.
All for currency. This line's poor

report. (The committee that met
with approval.) What's to say of what's
rambling, sportive of words: besides,
but not, if then. All for flim-flam,

all wrappings. Disaster-stricken leaves.
What missed doing? What under? What stand?

# Bell, Book, and Candle

To you, the carrier. To you, the old
bad tidings rounding the curve.
You with your almsgiving, your
oft-quoted sum. For you, there is less
reaching. For you, divinity in hand.
You, spat-shot shower. Blood-son. You,
firewalled armor. To you, the world
triangulated. You snort and you shrift.
You of the most for any cost. To
you, the pretty side faces. To you,
little do, little deed. For you, no one
calls out a warning. Onto you darkness
swift falls not saying your name.

# [The lady stirs]

## I

I'll to you: you used me and abused
me—what a tale to tear the heart
out of. The story that stories wind
around. I blazed death-skinned as a lily,
upgrounded in my gallowy, billowy veil.
The end a catapult cocked, nursed in hate.
I cousin to the cozener's fray. As any,
enemied. Too many to be numbered, but
they counted, and I marvelous less to be even
one. A priestly palmer gave the stake
with lips duende-sweet. *Ave, ave.* Here's
the little: I looked, I liked. Reckoning's past
bear, at bay and worn within my lark-laced
frock. The knowing known for naught.

## II

You'll to me: knowing not what I know
but a step out of turn. I misspoke:
I lost the name, spiced the pun,
and for it the outcome rains its pains
upon plaza stones. We havened a place
among the star-fetching high summer
weeds, away from the palmer with
his priestly grave stakes. Read the comet's
tail, unwisely won. The lilies burned,
the story tallowed. I went headlong
for sakes goodly though costly, medicined
by the pricking's point. I went along alone,
we with our oneness, we without which
the earth'd catch the spin of us undone.

## III

We'll to us: we are done for.
We have a motion to mar us.
None happier for the brief
aubade. Our larks against
us, the folly revenue our
fellows handed us. Here a half
of us, there a shadowcast
demeanor, our feet a heavy
lead. We marked the book
by wrong. We're barely a note
inside a song; we're a dust
mote alit in a comet's tail. We
with our tallies, our ranking
hearts lowed by the score.

# The Suit, a Letter

Oh, but there's nothing to get worked up over.
So there's another one in line, so there are others
who can make the queen blush. You and your
matchmaker's ornaments, the currency
of a cough, a guffaw. I've been observing
your glances, the curl of your lips. You're in good
company. A flower full of pockets pulled.
Smallness? That's for fleas. The woo is the way,
a bent head over books forecasting love's prophecy.
In miniature, I keep a picture, locked. Not some bleeding
heart on a sleeve, but a smith of the greatest kind. Forged
each letter to shape, the scripted slant of vowels rushed
out in a passion the sky can't color, sun blaze
any natural thing we were never meant to be.

# Rose

You were there to better me,
my goodness all rubbed out

as a mite. Such small cases
forwarded to a wider court

of rule. Bones buried deep
in the animal humus. I substituted

cause for caution. A tender
flower not, but stunted bud encased

full-calyx. Blossom to rot,
the fluke the measurements

mismarked. Rosetted by fault.
Broomed and witched. So much

for trained reach, for the upper
cased, for wider throw, red lip to

fall a dark shadowy under-eye.
Leaf to spot. Gnarled ashen base.

Overgrowth of green, sick-vigorous
vine, cane of split, off-shootings without

meaning, sickle-hooked to keep out.
I put you in the ornament, with

you for me for the prize. Some
take the cut to make one perfect.

# Superstition

But what with the knot in the rope's midsection?
What with the casket, the anchor of all?
Salted: as for accident. Stoned: as for
your body a tablet. Rose and crucifix
for the last finger pointing. Dogs
and their pack-hungriness. In time, cedars
harden by their own resin. As with each,
each door is numbered. A book of some
kind: moth-spotted, thumbed, closed.
Never a voice to call the night's hour, always
the owl that shakes nerves to part. But what
with the featherstitch under your rib cage?
What with your eyes that takes the dark to see?

# Siren Song

Baited it—that's what we did. One big
mess. Slick fat of a leopard seal, a mermaid
curse in inky waters, places we'll never
return to. I'm as part of the anchored
ship as any. I'm as reddened by hands
and murderously known. The songs
stars play clear out in the crystalline
heavens. Some lasting mention of the end
repeated each day we feast. When the seal
was hacked open, it thrashed first
like a bear, opened its jaw to show fangs
whiter than snow. We heaved it up. Suspended, it
looked priest-solemn, frozen in wondrous
content we'll never have. My saints
above me forgave nothing. We dread things.
We met the greater without cause or care.

# A Tundra of Misapplications

When to the coniferred hectares, vale to timberline, when
to the inland sea, there set in a stir...

They with sweet-sweet pleadings, all with eyes drawn by charcoal.

First, the firs chipped down to figural forms—mermaid, a bear
after mayflies, wolverine, a babushka hunched and mean.

> *Went to the shores as promised.*
> *The lake was our fill was us.*

The small lot grew to swell; the lake-crinkled
mud gave way. Then the larch fell

blanched, the rest to pulp. So they said,

this wasn't part of the contract; so it was transplant
the tagged to some other plot.

> *Took to the log and splint, took*
> *to the dampers and kettle,*
> *guarded as she-wolves we paced.*

Along came further white, full winter
in a wicked split. Our hearts wore out the ice.

They middled the mooncalf, dog seals strung tip
to tip. They of the brace. Of the grip.

*Buckets of pyrite, buckets of ore.*
*We haul back to strain. A hook and a lug.*


Before, we were copper filled with sun.
Before, thrush-throated, poured into:

> *His mother was a crevice,*
> *his father a speckled burbot fish . . .*


Our thoughts we stashed in the mountains,
our tongues looped in a curl. Such slurry

for the thick of us. Not even a storm could raise a noise.

If the smattering clouds weren't always present,
if the press-iron blankness weren't a nine-month's devotion. . . .


> *We'd be gale-swept, tinder-rooted our toes*
> *to the ground. We'd go in head first,*
>
> *the sapphired water, the rocky lake floor*
> *bottom. Water-laden and home.*

# [The nature of bad news infects the teller]

Ran out like a swift fin. Ran out
without turn or commotion. Night's
harried face heaved in mine. My heart-laden

feet galloped forward. The wind with
its thievery took out my breath. In time,
the length self-subtracted. Fronted, guardsmen

ushered me in. Had ribs picked clean to get it
out, had lung spurt, had *morte* attending
the background. The outcry was enough.

The carried thing had charms.
They went flush with blood, gripped
to the handle they flew. I knew

myself as terminal—my one reward.
Paid for by blows and bore it all.

# Timbered

Round and round they go
      with a ribbon and garlanded
            flowers in hand.

The bark won't unravel,
      the tree spells solidness—we
            grand, oaken, elmed selves

of the ancients. Our pith
      is clean. There's no pining
            away for tomorrow, we are

in current respiration,
      we move with the wind.
            Singular, we are

stunning. In horde,
      we are dense, differing
            dream. The autumnal

flashiness these days
      is drought-determined.
            We barely go beyond

the red. Our hollows
      are never vacant. We live
            to board; we take

the ax. Marbled inside
      the original stem. We were
            born we don't know when.

## To Pasture

Everywhere is a nowhere,
and here we are
in the middle of it.

For as long as we
could we galloped through
the cross-hatched daisies,

threw out our lungs
from the limestone
bluffs. The streams ran

long with a clay-jammed
soft bottom. Flood plains
turned for the richest

yield. It stunk high-fish,
green enough to breathe.
Sky was all

circumference, bell, or
curve, or big empty.
As with you. The husk-

wrecked dusks,
the nights where
I am where I am.

# Dispatch: At a Limp, Not at a Gallop

Dear Little Storm Cloud—

An onward push, that's the message I'm to send. The diamondback have their outcrop three days from you, and you're to wind along the river bluffs with an eye east. There'll be redstone and terror. Trees with scabby-white bark. Ground fox burrow near the rooted-out fell. I'm not one to powder my words, so know this: the plains take on innocence; that's their way of having you. Sun's got wide arc, the expanse beyond thought. The grass-flats have been known to swirl, to switch names, and even there all animals look the same. You're for the rough, know this. I'll make my report, keep you charted. I've set you up, now you make do.

Yours—without the bitterly—ushering,
Broken Feather

# Stuffed and Strung Up for the Birds

Shame—and that's the word
of rule. Even in the clear blue
afternoon I'm giving a lie to live
for. There's truth and half-truth;
there's fib and slant and white
in the center of the ever-blooming
roses. I talk it beyond compare:
freckled, horizon-eyed, straw
hair that sights a stuffed dummy head.
No escaping the hanging, there's
the time between sun's set
and the rupture of rise. So there's
a way to get out, I'm told, so
order me a dozen stand-ins.
I'm for score reductions, half-
points. I barely keep toes pointed
but the pointedness remains. Straight
and tidy as the alphabet. I don't know
why I'm staying here. The wind
is going around in circles; the dirt
in the heat gives up eddies
which have more beauty than I
could make. Lucky stars, I'm told
to say, bishop of the corn, out in
the expansive open, alone to my
thoughts, a wild-roaming dog
not in my dreams but in the bad ones.

# [How easy is a bush supposed a bear]

We forested forward, all the vegetation
agleam with wax-shine, the flaring eyes

of animals half-hidden, half-imaginary.
Some flowering weed somewhere released

its sick-sweet scent. There shapes
and there shapes. Sticks' crack and rustle

kept us tense for a chase. We turned
skittishness to play—a game of wits,

chicken-set, out-nerved. The rocks cut
faces, trees to limbs. We tended to clip

hearts, to cluster. Fear-fevered we turned
against what we knew: that is, one

another. Then, we made ourselves
each a boulder, perched uneasily

in our rigged garb. Toward morning, a mist
stilled the field in gray wash. A clarity

of form that early hour. A dove called
out *cooOOoo-woo-woo woooo*. I was no one's

in the dew-minted long grass, a return
to the familiar. We brushed off

our coats and everything else. I was
young and uninvolved anyway.

Ready excuse—I was never the same.

# Aubade

There's loneliness and there's this—
an unfrequented song, a startling voice
across years. A shifting position, hymn
from the hard bench, sharp something in
there, glass-glinted. If the movement
of trees in the weather front were enough.
If the notes were off-pitch but piercing
(which they are) as birdcall across
the stirring hour. In the woods,
a rustling of creatures we have no
idea of. Outcrops of limestone, wet leaves
lush and deadly. There's a time for killing,
some tell us, in the corner
of the who-knows-whereabouts. Everywhere,
the roadside lilies in thick morning
dew open orange and in numbers, one
after the other. Sun so strange it's as
though our looking, for a time, is first.

# Cloudland

You must not blame me
    if I talk to the clouds.
They have their own faces, their own

    leaks and splits, deceptive
as any gauzy substance tends
    to be. I took myself upward;

I went hillside to follow. A mindset
    that needed airing,
mud-stained tromp to the edge.

    Up above, a sort of
beyond-something-else. Climactic,
    atmospheric happenings.

There's little to say about
    clouds—they move on.
They don't care for the canopy,

    for scorch or drought.
They're part lake, part
    chemical compound.

Dispersive, discursive. I should
    be a mediator,
a meditator, a meteor; I should

    plummet and burn and be,
above all, a peaceful
    unobtrusive thing. But I'm no

    better than these
inconstant, unfeeling
    blots. These of the scaled

purple-blue insubstance, rippled
   effect; these of the driven,
storm-stalked seeders. I talk to

the clouds as I talk
   to no one. I talk to the clouds
as though I had earth to shun.

# Stock, Still

And so the counting became its own affair. A mix-up of apparent
circumstances, the humdrum notices of receipt and return and
return. Frost-marked mornings. Autumn evident in the trees
though the sky clear outside belief. I resorted to back-tracking. Trails
with their pack dust, and the creek reeking of cow or large
animal-wash. Burrs and hook-filled things of hate that attach to
dig in. I put one next to the other. I put each solid bundle of no-goodness
side-by-side. Hours and their unremarkable quality. Pinecones'

scaled structure, the weird blue berries of the tree of the dead. Hawks
in soar for spotting. This, for cycles of sun, of moon, of ground turning
cold and body turning cold. I never thought hard thoughts possible.
No inventory of leaves, no procedure of how they fall or what
they cover. There was self-concern long before there was empathy, one
beast might say to another. A prowling instinct. I am no other than this.

[ IV ]

# [If they would yield us but the superfluity while it were wholesome]

The steps were cold—
an ancient cold. We huddled
in lines that wound

through city streets. Stores
boarded with ply, as empty as our
traded-in gloves and shoes.

Mostly we cooperated; most
of the jostling happened behind.
Our hearts, fixed forward, gave off

a royal-blue affection. The scale
tipped this way and that: in one
pan clay; in the other, a pyramid

of faceted gems. We were the eyes,
we were weight shifted
foot to foot. This was a capital

moment. The mechanism, armed,
wavered; springs twitched
to settle. Even fortune mixed swords

and scales, fear and favor.
What would never be ours
hung in the balance.

# Monarchy

There was no room for us to have feelings.
Under the Queen, we were foiled, our faces blanked of wonder.
A pitiful ordeal, our cheap toil. We hated her for stealing.

Our crooked backs ached; our knees bled from kneeling,
the whole sum of our treasures given up to fund her.
There was no room for us to have feelings,

so we made our way quietly; we arranged our own dealings,
checked what we clocked. Each swallowed their thunder
and railed within. Nothing left out for stealing.

But pound for pound, we grew skinny, weary, reeling
from the new rules she devised. We had to watch and mind her.
There was no room for us to have feelings.

We were audited, then fined. We abided her schooling.
Then, all music stopped. All solitude filled, we couldn't ponder
our losses. We tried to forget how much she was stealing.

Our patron saints left us; the stars took to jeering, leering
at our lessened state. We hardened at our blunder.
There was no room to have any feelings.
What of us? Not a pittance. No worth there for stealing.

# [Yet let me have the substance rough, not the shadow]

And so there was a desperate edge.
A playschool line of obedience
that no longer applied. Talk smeared
across the board. I was into commotion
just like the rest. The rain's spate, the now-bare
trees befouled the streets with waste.
A tailless dog nosed around. The truth
was in the making, so we took to letting
out our cuffs. We made good audience.
Adhered to the ration, to making do
with a bloodless scene. Hushed all together.
Enter the one who licks and stoops; enter
the one who hands his name around;
enter the false prophet with genuine
zirconia eyes (knee-bender, self-puffer).
And to follow, the larger influx
of stuff—the box store closings,
the hand for a hug for a cold shoulder.
Our selves went to scatter. Elongated
the blame, wiped in the dirt what names
one could. Look: try as you might you can't
replicate this. You'll be nothing but adequate.
Coins have been tossed, backsides
shined, and the last fields reaped
of their corn. The mixed-up weather,
bats and bees virally dropping. Moon
in descent. The grasshopper rubs
its violin wings as the frost hardens.
There was a splitting down the middle.

# Solar Complaint

Sun, you have your own combustion, storm

glow and flare, spots on each quadrant. Filtered
process, the plant-soak of your gaze. Rise/set: given

divine name, center, torch that is no torch,
moon-fodder. Quarter you

and there's gaseous goo, hydrogen core, the mess
of what we don't know inside. You've got pull,

you've shade, your eclipse antics, artful
sense of new. All metal's fire in refraction, mirror

of image and squint. A gadget to take
the polar caps apart (given the greening

conditions). Grass-feed, time-base, our
skin yours. Get this—you're hot,

your Apollo-swoon, wax conditioning. Sand
scorched, flood of sharp and bleach. Thought you

a constant, rule-driven. No, you cool
and interrupt. Coronal material, a mock-

you ("why dost thou thus"), an effect.

# Lunar Complaint

Moon, you are a button-hole anus! Moon, you plagiarize
the sun! Blue-blotched and lidded, a doodad
repeated in phases, slivered as a fingernail, globular

as batter dropped on a griddle. Your half-
veiled tease, a frenzied mob scouring the village,
pheromone-drunk deer sniffing each other

out during the night's peak. Overall, an influence
that's moderate: tidal sway, the wolf's bay, the changeling
a no-no in the shepherd's handbook. A tag-along

from the start. Oh, to be cheese! To rave as a lunatic
under your submarine stillness! Moon, you beam
unmystical, a nickel in the Milky Way's pocket. Subsidized

by lovers, trophy at the end of the race. Too easily
feminized, calendared: your esoterica, your shoehorn
form. So what with your wax and wane? Inconstancy's

rental. Selenocentrics have it wrong: predictable,
a false lodestar, your emulations a tinwork art.
You are not the thing to match or the eye to become.

# [Cut is the branch that might have grown full straight]

Take this to heart, you scholars of misintent:

I am to burn not only the books, but the sky
full stream of meteors that fall as they fall

when man abides the unlawful. Justice
is marked so. By increments. By angles.

The turn of a wheel. There's one

who takes notice, one who takes
advantage. So by the boughs overladen

with autumn-past fruit. Near frost: yellow

by withering. So by the bow the archer
strung with heart's aim and doe

downed by higher cunning. Liquid eyes

the goddess might inhabit. Soft brown
hide that is anything but my earlier form.

Aligned by degree. Decree of insight,

some partiality of what before
was charged with meaning. To practice any

gesture of wonder would unking my seat

here in the high glory stakes, mine
for reaching. Hellish to plummet, no doubt:

the place we know ourselves. Unfortuned.

# King of the Boars

I said, "Excuse me," and you said, "Draw."
I said, "God's a day," and you spat, "For a whore."
"Pleased be you," I said with crowning smile;
"To piss on your leg," you finished with a flourish
of spray. "I'm beyond this world," I tried
to explain, angelic of expression. "I'm king
of the boars," you boasted, debuting a horned stick,
lips curled. "In service to all," I bowed with a cross
etched across my heart. "In for the larger sum then,"
you said knowingly, with a jerked motion
of your pants. I downed a soft frown, "You are the lamb
that wanders off, but knows its way," and opened
my arms. "Better a bucket for the ham, a stool
for the scrub," you scoffed, fingers knived
to the throat. "No sacrifice too small," I
said straight to the eye. "You salve and you patch,
all kissy where it counts," you lashed, flushed high
across the cheeks. I was starting to lose my temper:
"Off with you then, you minion, you crupper!"
"Ah," you said, bitter-tendered at last, "you flip
the switch when the heart should be steadfast."

# Two-Bit Song

What more pointed than a trout on a spear?
What more grotesque than the grosser

end exposed? What else
mushy as peas? What sog and slop?

What tattling talk at tea? Home's abliss.
Buds throw off their tresses, the hedgerows

evened in new green. Sheep, dots in the distance.
Cows a tail flap with their milky

means. All the roads lead. This instant's
a false one. What couldn't be more

glorious than the lover gored at dawn?
What sad letter for the sad, sad doorstep

receiver? The step and its concreteness.
What more yellow than the daffodilly leveled

low by rain? A grassy tender spot.
Bugleweed of the mat

and the spike. Inherited proceedings,
one after another after another.

What's apt to soil? What art to foil?
What foul weather for the one at a loss?

What with the whatings? As if
the question itself made remedy.

# [But yet I run before my horse to market]

A serious mishappening, you misshapen
mopish malingerer. To have motioned
the morning's mirrored minnowing, small
pond that is your mind. You muck. You mistake
me. Mocked by measure. Keep your molten
silver-minked miniver, masquerading misfits.
I've a matter to mar you. I'll meander on
your menacing mien. Minion to your merriment,
married to the moored mission. You, I mitt
for a misinformer. Miscreant, moldering
as a muskrat. Make you a merchant? Should I
money up your mansion more? Make monkey
to your mistress? Might I mix the music to marvel
your majesty? Make haste to the mistletoe? Must
I mean well? I'm one of a mortalized many. I mime
the most macabre. I will not miss you.

# [As I have done the rest of my misleaders]

## I

This was the year we spent pent on woe.
Not so at the start. We packed a swollen parcel,
our growth twofold, steadily eyed. You
off riotous among the pipers, myself
a hatched case brooding along the brook-side.
I envied you your advantage. The take, meager
dividends that filled a sugar-sack of tens. We
were unmoored. We rugged up the alleys, bartered
the castle stone for timbered cheer. Swanned around
our name. I let you know your place: pond-scum, filler
fish, stick-in-the-mud. You, for yours, pinned me
the apparent, blood, the expectancy. I jollied
good-natured, a truant through and through. To each
we were true. For a time. Despite this, we aged.

## II

We bent ourselves to truth. The agéd ends
to which we did not adhere. Valor by position
as the clouds atop the hillside shrive the tree.
We wanted more. The past golden by our
remembrance. My life to you a doved
remainder I did not need. There for a fill. A lad
upon your knee, I saw you at your railing
best: the covenant too holy, the cross a bear
to chest. We littled our woe, pieced by the cup.
I wondered, who else could we be? A field's worth
of distance. You unsunned; me unsung, graced
out in portions. Once was a piper…but I quieted.
Winter-scarped our time to end. I had
an uncommon vision; you commoned it,
needing me. A term with which I no longer agree.

[ V ]

# Prop Rockery Reprised

Above all, we were tired
of making lists. The work

filed us away; we acted
listless as the auburn leaves.

Sun-blanched and manic. The season
ended in stalemate. Our own

legs pulled, a method torturous
as arithmetic. Easy answers

led to those less so. We tightened
our shoestrings. The air

opened as though a permanent exit.
Tree-lined streets gave way to more

destination than we could afford
to go. Immaculate Sunday with grass too

good for a picnic. These were
not our only troubles.

# Albatross

After the bow and the dance, a going
on and on. The broad plain unbroken
except by wind. I never had enough
in me; I never had a we in me. We
are such starts and ill-fits. I give up
north, shell to the south the flotsam
float scum. We in our sentences
of gloom and doom, of the perfect pair.
The sea's template, ridged. There a sheer
drop, plunge, there layers not to split
or see. Being this soft tissue, a wideness
that matters only when set against another.
Being this: little sense, nautical and numb.

# Accumulation Song

*If you add a little to a little, and then do it again,*
*soon that little shall be much.*
—Hesiod

Some obsessions operate by default,
some by the natural aperture
of the brain. A clock palmed within
the nervous system, the very

fingertips and extension of digits
racked up like a confessor. Pulled,
and the rip a wreckage wave-thrown,
gutted. Sweats to take the pit

out, an increasing. Movement
as solemn as heartbeat. Again and
unthoughtfully again. Then there's
the counting of years from end

to end (forty-seven, ninety-three).
A short breath till there's none. One
illusion: it'll never run out. Without,
there's no reason to mean.

# A Final Procession for the Pattern Maker

How young we are to mind
ourselves in the matter—young
in the acts, young in the manner
to give ourselves up, to determine
ourselves over.
           With a scope
to the printwork, we unloop
the scroll. Plum-red richness
in fabric, threading to pleating.
Rigid in collar, the laced graced
with missing.
           How keen are we
to arrange the ruffles, the damasks
of turning vine and rose, those
ornaments satined and sealed up
forever. How angry the clasp, how
pinned-down
           the final answer.
Robed for the makers, a face
best painted by late summer's
gold twilight. In any tree, a body;
in any costume, a ghost.
           How odd:
are we to know enough—plunge,
cut, remainder? How old, how little,
how dressed for comfort? Off in the end:
no last word, no second offer.

# The Songless Ha-Ha

*After Aggie Zed*

Unlike the one that says, "First we sell them
anything," in which an unfinished man points

a gun into the hard ribbed side of the horse reared up
on hind legs, belly exposed, forefront and head

zeroed by a cloud smoke-black—this painting
has two horses. They run the thick middle

field, within a mess of color and smear (what
the hand was doing then, all without). They

horizontal the everywhere, these two, full-
winded to range out the dead white surrounding

space. It is from this, the human outline looks
at them. On all fours more paw than palm,

his muteness draws them perpetually away
from us. They'll not come closer for long.

# [I was not made a horse]

Up-split as a wick. That quick.
   First flare. Outshone
the crackpots, their rags
   a-stitched, a-new, all a-gold.
We were better than
   this: the river's sop, the breach
and spill, everything mush galore.
   Nature's false metaphors. No less
a forced self singled from a we. Demand
   turned lighter head. Uncrowned.
Unlaureled. Left with a wall built
   by common hands, and a dusty
glassed light that was not. Gray slate,
   cindered solidness that is me
inside a me inside. Ha! this chump's
   not kicking like he used to!
I've been re-shoed, frowned at
   by the crew. Upstaged, done
for. A place-set where I'm a spoon
   missing. Rails to rattles, hugs
for your ugly mug. There's a cheap
   side yet if you want me. . . .
I can say, "Used to be, used
   to be," with a grin. Took on words
with their *arch* and *ick*. Took
   on failure. God-sided,
spirit-quickened—so I was sold
   into. A breaking is in for.
I'll to my bit. I'll to a stirrup.
   Cued for the high score, the most
daring vault. My fault?
   I'm beyond even that. Look
what they say: the loose stone
   will bring the manor
down. Keep your chin back, head

straight. That's neck-breaking
speed we're into now. All
    a go, giddy and heya
for hollering. Hayers for
    hire. Criminal. I'm in
top form to take a walkabout.
    Literal. This is a wall
where I find my stand.
    This is a stand. This.

# [I can drink with any tinker]

I take my sore subject to the Star in Abingdon.

A high head full with more lily than gut.

The cup's foam, the swagger-talk, the ballad-paper thin walls.

That fellow on the heap pulls a lean look in from the laughing corner.

The josh is on him.

I'm a one person kind of person.

It's trash for the badgery-looking numskulls.

I'm best with the comebacks.

We're full of ailments. We're full of whatever.

Mildew grows in the wood.

I roam with a hiccup.

There was a long war behind me.

They cooked the goose.

All along I've behaved so well.

I let the hands go with the tongue.

# [The juggler casteth a mist to work the closer]

Left the game to run riot, a further school
      of abuse, of sorts. Trumpery to the finest,
a go-for-broke mass psychology, a clammy

handshake put to the test. Fell flat
      on our gourds, stumped
in the fair fields of fair mire. We donated our tricks,

bag for bag, tic for tic. Ah, what for craft! What
      for a melody, the path to love!
It's not what the spoilers play, that dumb fuck-for-fuck's

sake, that "see-what-I-did-when-you-weren't-looking"
      underhand way. A well-placed
peel, a pawn's advance for the steal. Would like to take

on more. Another throw. This's what we're for.
We flip plurals by the thumb; we favor no one.

# Ballad of the Face in the Rock

It's the flatness that stills us.
No more tumbles, no more falls.
We're numb at zero, in plain
sight of the wind. Then, more
wind. Then, the hard-factored sky.

————

What do we know? Not the answers,
not the age-old bones of the petrified
pines. Steady and rooted. How do we make
shapes out of our limited sight? The ferns
and their unfurling out. A form that is
form without. A form thought structured.

————

So many stories, they tell us, within us.
We roll words we've hoarded,
heavy from disuse. We take in the sky
darkened by the afterthought
of the sun. We slow our tongues; we're
cold and dull. We harbor such things:
weight and many etceteras.

————

We're a rock face of names, arranged
in three columns. Quieted, nearly. No doors
to walk out of except one.

———

Nothing soft exists. We're equally worn
by the day's rotation.

We can be perfect: cloven, drossed, sanded.
Dust. Oh, we can be.


———


We're not a smart set. We
mismatch the elements. half

of us hot, half not. Feldspar portioned
by milky quartz. Mineral, part of.

We're here with our one voice
all centuries.

# [Let me be thought too busy in my fears]

So it fell out like this—
went to the edge of daybreak: a golden gulf
racked with fog. There, the earth grew older;

there, the birds tweep't their little riches
from the brambly crisscross of hawthorn.
It was a jaspered moment, a mutt formation,

an incremental hue upon hue. I fit myself
inward, a spleen-racked mind to be better, a knack
for staging the upsets, the empire. I turned

my innocent side out, knavery's plain face,
and fessed up to my brothers. They were sap filled
to the heart: because love's its own embargo,

a charted unknown, self-painted in selfsame
colors; because fear-flung they squander.
I made a mock-hobby of the elect. I played

to their heel; I planted the itch. They sat, pups
to my lips, whelped by their rule of seize
and plunder. Then, night turned out day, and,

in short, there was an earth crash,
a backlash, and now I'm chained
as a liar. A flinty streak with no fire.

# Finale

There was a plan for exit, it was called:
"Swan Song of the Rock in the Sling."
"Adieu," said the girl from her riverbed;
"So long," chimed the duo of clowns.
Somewhere the clink of a leaking faucet, outside
a Niagara of thick summer air. The show unraveled
as a series of head-scratches, capped with a punch
that soured in age. I was geared for applause
and promotion; you took to the boot,
the toad, and the fawn. Modesty's its own
advertisement, the free-for-all a false doubling
with us locked at the knee. I decked the lawn
with a gauze of finery; you set springs
to catch woodcocks. I gave a jab, you a snip;
I a dig, you a fib. We stood cheek to cheek
amidst the foliage of our misdeeds. On the plains,
a cracking open; on the home front, the newly blasted
territories divvied up for greed. From then on,
the gold wore teeth marks; from then on, the coal
smoked the trees. We felt the demotion
as rubble: we backfill, we sediment. An avalanche,
the final curtain. We look to learn. We went forward as one.

# Notes

[I]

"Prop Rockery": "looped and windowed raggedness" from William Shakespeare's *King Lear*.

[In thy dumb action will I be as perfect]: Title from Shakespeare's *Titus Andronicus*.

[All with me's meet that I can fashion fit]: Title from Shakespeare's *King Lear*.

[Like boys unto a muss kings would start forth]: Title from Shakespeare's *Antony and Cleopatra*.

[Time and the hour runs through the roughest day]: Title from Shakespeare's *Macbeth*.

[So that they seeme, and covet not to be]: Title from George Gascoigne's *The Steele Glas*. This poem owes much to Rayna Kalas's article, "The Technology of Reflection: Renaissance Mirrors of Steel and Glass" (*Journal of Medieval and Early Modern Studies* 32:3, Fall 2002).


[II]

[Accoutred as I was I plungèd in]: Title from Shakespeare's *Julius Caesar*.

"Tract Song": Epigraph from Francis Bacon's essay "Of Truth."

"Mare's Nest": *mare's nest*—i. A hoax or fraud; ii. An extraordinarily complicated situation. In November 2004, Congress reversed a thirty-year government policy that protected all wild horses. The new law allowed for rounded up horses and burros, and those animals older than ten years or those that failed to be adopted, to be sold for slaughter. Denise Levertov on Emily Dickinson (*The Letters of Robert Duncan and Denise Levertov*. Ed. Robert J. Bertholf and Albert Gelpi. Stanford: Stanford University Press, 2003). "Not to commend, but to set it" is derived from Dickinson's July 1862 letter to Thomas Wentworth Higginson: "Men do not call the surgeon to commend the bone, but to set it, sir, and fracture within is more critical." The nursery rhyme, "Hark, hark, the dogs bark," dates back to thirteenth-century England and has a mixed history and origin, but it's often associated with the wandering minstrels who might have used such lyrics to communicate messages of dissent.

[The world is deceived with ornament]: Title from Shakespeare's *The Merchant of Venice*.

[The lady stirs]: Title from Shakespeare's *Romeo and Juliet*.


[III]

"A Tundra of Misapplications": *"His mother was a crevice, his father a speckled burbot fish"* is from a Russian folktale about three water-babies born in Lake Baikal.

[The nature of bad news infects the teller]: Title from Shakespeare's *Antony and Cleopatra*.

[How easy is a bush supposed a bear]: Title from Shakespeare's *A Midsummer Night's Dream*.

"Cloudland": Borrows a line from Henry David Thoreau, "You must not blame me if I do talk to the clouds."


[IV]

[If they would yield us but the superfluity while it were wholesome]: Title from Shakespeare's *Coriolanus*.

[Yet let me have the substance rough, not the shadow]: Title from John Marston's *The Scourge of Villany* (1599).

"Solar Complaint": "why dost thou thus" from John Donne's "The Sun Rising."

[Cut is the branch that might have grown full straight]: Title from Christopher Marlowe's *Doctor Faustus*.

[But yet I run before my horse to market]: Title from Shakespeare's *Richard III*.

[As I have done the rest of my misleaders]: Title from Shakespeare's *Henry IV, Part 1*.

[V]

[I was not made a horse]: Title from Shakespeare's *Richard II*.

[I can drink with any tinker]: Title from Shakespeare's *Henry IV, Part I*.

[The juggler casteth a mist to work the closer]: Title from Stephen Gosson's *School of Abuse* (1579).

[Let me be thought too busy in my fears]: Title from Shakespeare's *Othello*.

"Finale": "you set springs to catch woodcocks" from Shakespeare's *Hamlet*.